# LYFE-ISMS

## EVERYDAY QUOTES FOR EVERYDAY LIVING

Patrick Petit-Frere

BLUEPRINT PRESS
INTERNATIONALE

ISBN
978-1-959365-78-5 (Paperback)
978-1-959365-79-2 (eBook)

**To God.**

> *I thank God for saving me and planting within me the desire to love You with all my heart. Without You, I would have no purpose for living. You have given me an assignment, and that is to draw the masses to Jesus. To my God and my King, I pray that You are pleased with this project.*

**To my wife.**

> *I would like to take this time to celebrate the love of my life, Pascalle. You have supported me in all my endeavors. Thank you for being the real individual that you are. This project is for you, babe.*

**To my kids.**

> *Elan, Zion, and Hannah, I am honored that God chose me to be your father. My prayer is that you guys will not only apply the gems in this book, but also pass Lyfe-isms down to your children. I love you all with every fiber of my being. This book is for you.*

**To my mom and dad, Rev. Verma & Lady Marie Petit-Frere.**

   *All I have to say are three words: I owe you. You know exactly what that means. Thank you for praying for me when I was away from the things of God. I believe that I am the man that I am because you believed God for total transformation. There is a huge crown awaiting both of you in glory. This book is for you.*

**To Anne Garcon, Ruth Jeanty, Vanessa Vixama and Cliff Jean-Pierre.**

   *I thank you for helping with the formatting of Lyfe-isms. Your contribution will forever be appreciated. May God add to you blessing and favor. This book is for you, guys.*

# Table of Contents

# Introduction to Lyfe-Isms

Wisdom is available to those who have ears to hear and eyes to see. One of the major reasons why many of us make poor decisions in life is because we lack wisdom. The Bible tells us in Proverbs 1:20, "Wisdom cries without; she utters her voice in the streets." To me, this means that wisdom tries to grab our attention daily. The question is, are we hearing and seeing the life lessons that are being presented to us?

Lyfe-ims are my personal values that I attempt to practice daily. These principles are all rooted in the Word of God, which I believe is the foundation from which we ought to draw wisdom. In writing Lyfe-ims, my aspired goal is to pass these life quotes down to the next generation of leaders and trailblazers. In the Bible, there is a passage which speaks of a generation that arose of whom did not know the works of God (Judges 2:10). Some may say, how is that even possible? Well, we see this epidemic happening in our day.

Lyfe-isms was written with the intention of pointing people to the power and nature of God, through the person of His son, Jesus Christ. My hope is that Lyfe-isms will cause many to see their need for wisdom, and as a result, they will run to Jesus. Above all, my prayer is that after reading these quotes, you will "Find Lyfe In Every Line."

Patrick Petit-Frere

**Prov. 19:20** Listen to advice and accept discipline, and at the end you will be counted among the wise.

# Faith/Hope

Mark 11:22 "Have faith in God," Jesus answered.

According to the Bible, faith is defined as such; "The substance of things hoped for and the evidence of things not seen"(Hebrews 11:1). It is also defined as "complete trust or confidence in someone or something". For the Christian, faith is our "Lyfeline." In fact, one cannot embrace the implications of Christianity if they do not possess faith. Faith and hope work hand in hand. We have faith for what we hope for.

Hope is a feeling of expectation and desire for a certain thing to happen. Therefore, faith is the vehicle which takes me to the very thing I am hoping for. The Bible says, "without faith it is impossible to please God (Hebrews 11:6)." Do you have a desire to please God? Are you undergoing certain trials that are challenging your faith? Well this chapter will spark, inspire, and ignite within you the faith that you need to accomplish what God has designed for you to carry out. My prayer is that you will find "Lyfe In Every Line."

Your life may be upside down. Jesus has the
power to turn your life right-side up.

Reflection: What does this mean to you?

_____

_____

_____

_____

_____

_____

_____

Application: How can you apply this to your life? OR How will you apply
this to your life?

_____

_____

_____

_____

_____

God may not tell you where you are going, but
He will order your steps as you go.


Reflection: What does this mean to you?

_____

_____

_____

_____

_____

_____


Application: How can you apply this to your life? OR How will you apply
this to your life?

_____

_____

_____

_____

_____

Don't think that the trial you are facing is pointless. God is allowing it to play as a spiritual GPS. He realizes that when we are up, we don't usually seek Him as we should. He, therefore, allows trials to come to redirect our attention and affection back to Him.

Reflection: What does this mean to you?

_____

_____

_____

_____

_____

_____

Application: How can you apply this to your life? OR How will you apply this to your life?

_____

_____

_____

_____

_____

_____

Storms are no respecter of persons.

Reflection: What does this mean to you?

_____

_____

_____

_____

_____

_____

Application: How can you apply this to your life? OR How will you apply this to your life?

_____

_____

_____

_____

_____

_____

"Trust in the plan God has for you." Many of us plan out our lives and expect God to cosign it. It's not too late to put your plans in the hands of Jesus. This is an exhortation to whomever has an ear to hear. In case you missed the message, allow me to repeat what I hear in the spirit:"TRUST IN THE PLAN GOD HAS FOR YOU."

Reflection: What does this mean to you?

_____

_____

_____

_____

_____

Application: How can you apply this to your life? OR How will you apply this to your life?

_____

_____

_____

_____

_____

Do not make a move without consulting the Father.

Reflection: What does this mean to you?

_____

_____

_____

_____

_____

_____

Application: How can you apply this to your life? OR How will you apply this to your life?

_____

_____

_____

_____

_____

_____

My God never faints. My God never sleeps, nor slumbers. He is watching over the word He spoke over your life. He is faithful to perform and execute what He promised in His time, not ours.

Reflection: What does this mean to you?

_____

_____

_____

_____

_____

Application: How can you apply this to your life? OR How will you apply this to your life?

_____

_____

_____

_____

_____

Be still in the presence of God and allow Him to lead and direct
your life. Relinquish your will and submit to His. He is trying
to take you to a place called rest. So just rest in Him today.

Reflection: What does this mean to you?

_____

_____

_____

_____

_____

_____

Application: How can you apply this to your life? OR How will you apply
this to your life?

_____

_____

_____

_____

_____

Wisdom is crying out loud and clear, hoping
someone will grab hold of its lessons.

Reflection: What does this mean to you?

_____

_____

_____

_____

_____

Application: How can you apply this to your life? OR How will you apply
this to your life?

_____

_____

_____

_____

_____

What you desire for yourself,
God may desire something different.

Reflection: What does this mean to you?

_____

_____

_____

_____

_____

Application: How can you apply this to your life? OR How will you apply this to your life?

_____

_____

_____

_____

_____

Move in the direction of what God promised you.

Reflection: What does this mean to you?

_____

_____

_____

_____

_____

_____

Application: How can you apply this to your life? OR How will you apply this to your life?

_____

_____

_____

_____

_____

_____

Knowing you have to "let it go" and actually doing
it, are two completely different things.

Reflection: What does this mean to you?

_____

_____

_____

_____

_____

_____

Application: How can you apply this to your life? OR How will you apply
this to your life?

_____

_____

_____

_____

_____

_____

Encouragement has the ability to lift a weary soul.

Reflection: What does this mean to you?

_____

_____

_____

_____

_____

_____

Application: How can you apply this to your life? OR How will you apply this to your life?

_____

_____

_____

_____

_____

_____

Father, into your hands, I commit my will.

Reflection: What does this mean to you?

_____

_____

_____

_____

_____

_____

Application: How can you apply this to your life? OR How will you apply this to your life?

_____

_____

_____

_____

_____

Perseverance: Trusting God when life makes no sense.

Reflection: What does this mean to you?

_____

_____

_____

_____

_____

Application: How can you apply this to your life? OR How will you apply this to your life?

_____

_____

_____

_____

_____

Do what the Lord tells you to do. Here Ye Him, not the opinions of "them." You have more in you than you know. The only way to achieve all that you were destined for, is to weed out the naysayers and keep your gaze upward.

Reflection: What does this mean to you?

_____

_____

_____

_____

_____

Application: How can you apply this to your life? OR How will you apply this to your life?

_____

_____

_____

_____

_____

_____

Fix your eyes to the hills because your help is
found nowhere else, but in the Lord.

Reflection: What does this mean to you?

_____

_____

_____

_____

_____

Application: How can you apply this to your life? OR How will you apply
this to your life?

_____

_____

_____

_____

_____

Give God your weakness,
and He'll give you his strength.

Reflection: What does this mean to you?

_____

_____

_____

_____

_____

Application: How can you apply this to your life? OR How will you apply this to your life?

_____

_____

_____

_____

_____

# Love

Colossians 3:14 And over all these virtues put on love, which binds them all together in perfect unity.

L ove is a word that we throw around loosely. Most people misappropriate the concept of love because they have not encountered the essence of love. The Bible tells us that God is love (1 John 4:8). The dilemma this world encounters is that we are trying to love without God. When we embrace the love that God has for us, we will then operate in that same love towards our neighbors, family and friends.

Are you struggling with loving people at school, work or even church? The love of God will bring peace where conflict resides. We are told in the Bible to put on love (Col.3:14). The only way to put on this kind of love, is if we are prepared to receive the love the Father has extended to us, through His Son Jesus Christ. This chapter will expose you to quotes on love that will, by God's grace, challenge you to live and walk in the love of God. Be blessed as you dive in, and allow the love of God to overwhelm your heart.

God is speaking. Do you hear Him? He's saying
that He loves you with an everlasting love.


Reflection: What does this mean to you?

_____

_____

_____

_____

_____


Application: How can you apply this to your life? OR How will you apply
this to your life?

_____

_____

_____

_____

_____

Love covers many flaws.

Reflection: What does this mean to you?

_____

_____

_____

_____

_____

_____

Application: How can you apply this to your life? OR How will you apply this to your life?

_____

_____

_____

_____

_____

We need to learn to celebrate our peers' accomplishments instead of trying to "steal" their moment. I say, if everyone lives with an attitude of esteeming others more highly than themselves, Christianity would be more appealing.

Reflection: What does this mean to you?

_____

_____

_____

_____

_____

_____

Application: How can you apply this to your life? OR How will you apply this to your life?

_____

_____

_____

_____

_____

_____

Let your words be someone's Lyfeline today.

Reflection: What does this mean to you?

_____

_____

_____

_____

_____

_____

Application: How can you apply this to your life? OR How will you apply this to your life?

_____

_____

_____

_____

_____

_____

Fight hate with love.

Reflection: What does this mean to you?

_____

_____

_____

_____

_____

_____

Application: How can you apply this to your life? OR How will you apply this to your life?

_____

_____

_____

_____

_____

Can't Hate on Love.

Reflection: What does this mean to you?

_____

_____

_____

_____

_____

_____

Application: How can you apply this to your life? OR How will you apply this to your life?

_____

_____

_____

_____

_____

Give the Lord a chance to show you how much He loves you. We rather live outside of His influence, than in His presence. God wants to love on you with His grace.

Reflection: What does this mean to you?

_____

_____

_____

_____

_____

Application: How can you apply this to your life? OR How will you apply this to your life?

_____

_____

_____

_____

_____

God grieves because He sees many of us walking to a place He didn't
design for us. Make your way back to His love and embrace.


Reflection: What does this mean to you?

_____

_____

_____

_____

_____

_____


Application: How can you apply this to your life? OR How will you apply
this to your life?

_____

_____

_____

_____

_____

_____

God is after your heart. Stay on the operating table and let
Him do what He does best. Too many believers are trying to
heal others when we are the ones in dire need of a healing.
He loves you dearly and wants to make you whole.

Reflection: What does this mean to you?

_____

_____

_____

_____

_____

Application: How can you apply this to your life? OR How will you apply
this to your life?

_____

_____

_____

_____

_____

Teach us how to live in unison.

Reflection: What does this mean to you?

_____

_____

_____

_____

_____

Application: How can you apply this to your life? OR How will you apply this to your life?

_____

_____

_____

_____

_____

God told us in His Holy Word that we are fearfully and wonderfully made. His Word should be sufficient for us to live life with heads lifted high. Embrace who God made you to be with or without cosigners.

Reflection: What does this mean to you?

_____

_____

_____

_____

_____

Application: How can you apply this to your life? OR How will you apply this to your life?

_____

_____

_____

_____

_____

Love God more than yourself.

Reflection: What does this mean to you?

_____

_____

_____

_____

_____

_____

Application: How can you apply this to your life? OR How will you apply this to your life?

_____

_____

_____

_____

_____

It is arrogant and prideful not to ask God for help. He is your source, and we ought to come to Him in times of need.

Reflection: What does this mean to you?

_____

_____

_____

_____

_____

Application: How can you apply this to your life? OR How will you apply this to your life?

_____

_____

_____

_____

_____

According to Jesus, you were a love worth dying for.

Reflection: What does this mean to you?

_____

_____

_____

_____

_____

_____

Application: How can you apply this to your life? OR How will you apply this to your life?

_____

_____

_____

_____

_____

_____

# Salvation

Psalm 62:1 Truly my soul finds rest in God;
my salvation comes from him.

O nce an individual receives Jesus as Lord over their lives, there is a certain conduct of living God desires for us to adopt. When God saves a person, He now owns that person. This means our lives no longer belong to us. We are now called and commissioned to live according to the standards of God. That standard is holiness, obedience and righteousness.

A person who has been saved from a destructive lifestyle, lives in gratitude to the one who saved them. In the Christian's case, we are forever grateful that God sent His Son to die a death that we deserved. In light of this death and sacrifice, we gladly conform to a new way of living. This chapter is filled with powerful convictions of a life submitted to the Lordship of Jesus Christ.

One of the main intentions/purposes of Lyfe-isms is to anchor and add a sense of stabilization, as it pertains to your walk with God. As you approach this section of the book, open your heart to accept exactly what the Lord would have you to receive.

I hear some people say that they are not ready to come to Jesus because they need to get themselves right. I say, come to Jesus and He'll make you right(eous).

Reflection: What does this mean to you?

_____

_____

_____

_____

_____

Application: How can you apply this to your life? OR How will you apply this to your life?

_____

_____

_____

_____

_____

Believe in the Lord Jesus and you will receive eternal life--not when you die, but as soon as you make the confession.

Reflection: What does this mean to you?

_____

_____

_____

_____

_____

_____

Application: How can you apply this to your life? OR How will you apply this to your life?

_____

_____

_____

_____

_____

_____

The glory costs. Are you willing to pay up?

Reflection: What does this mean to you?

_____

_____

_____

_____

_____

Application: How can you apply this to your life? OR How will you apply this to your life?

_____

_____

_____

_____

_____

If Jesus were to come today, will He ruin your plans
or would He be gracefully received? (Selah)

Reflection: What does this mean to you?

_____

_____

_____

_____

_____

_____

Application: How can you apply this to your life? OR How will you apply
this to your life?

_____

_____

_____

_____

_____

_____

Life is senseless if Jesus ain't in it.

Reflection: What does this mean to you?

_____

_____

_____

_____

_____

Application: How can you apply this to your life? OR How will you apply this to your life?

_____

_____

_____

_____

_____

This generation is in desperate need of transparent and authentic ministers. The days of doing ministry for the sake of filling up our itineraries, are over. People are dying spiritually, and the devil is not playing fair. From this day forward, let us really be about the glory of God, the edification of the saints, and less about the feeding of our egos.

Reflection: What does this mean to you?

_____

_____

_____

_____

_____

_____

Application: How can you apply this to your life? OR How will you apply this to your life?

_____

_____

_____

_____

_____

_____

This generation doesn't need another event. What we
need is a true encounter with the Lord Jesus.

Reflection: What does this mean to you?

_____

_____

_____

_____

_____

_____

Application: How can you apply this to your life? OR How will you apply
this to your life?

_____

_____

_____

_____

_____

The insecurity level of today's generation is at its all-time
high. Fall more in love with what God says about you
and less with what folks' opinion of you may be.


Reflection: What does this mean to you?

_____

_____

_____

_____

_____

_____


Application: How can you apply this to your life? OR How will you apply
this to your life?

_____

_____

_____

_____

_____

_____

Stop following man and start following the next move of God.

Reflection: What does this mean to you?

_____

_____

_____

_____

_____

Application: How can you apply this to your life? OR How will you apply this to your life?

_____

_____

_____

_____

_____

Jesus saves. Jesus heals. Jesus delivers. If you need any of these, run to Jesus. He will, by no means, cast you away.

Reflection: What does this mean to you?

_____

_____

_____

_____

_____

_____

Application: How can you apply this to your life? OR How will you apply this to your life?

_____

_____

_____

_____

_____

_____

To know God, through the person of His Son Jesus Christ,
is the greatest reward a man could ever receive.

Reflection: What does this mean to you?

_____

_____

_____

_____

_____

Application: How can you apply this to your life? OR How will you apply
this to your life?

_____

_____

_____

_____

_____

Fix your eyes on Jesus 'cause only He can save you.

Reflection: What does this mean to you?

_____

_____

_____

_____

_____

_____

Application: How can you apply this to your life? OR How will you apply this to your life?

_____

_____

_____

_____

_____

Hold on to Jesus... Cry out to Jesus... He will
save those who acknowledge Him.

Reflection: What does this mean to you?

_____

_____

_____

_____

_____

_____

Application: How can you apply this to your life? OR How will you apply
this to your life?

_____

_____

_____

_____

_____

_____

Give Jesus access to invade your life. Relinquish your
will today. He is looking for a surrendered life.

Reflection: What does this mean to you?

_____

_____

_____

_____

_____

_____

Application: How can you apply this to your life? OR How will you apply
this to your life?

_____

_____

_____

_____

_____

_____

Life without Jesus isn't life at all.

Reflection: What does this mean to you?

_____

_____

_____

_____

_____

_____

Application: How can you apply this to your life? OR How will you apply this to your life?

_____

_____

_____

_____

_____

_____

Sin has a heartbeat, and it beats to death.

Reflection: What does this mean to you?

_____

_____

_____

_____

_____

_____

Application: How can you apply this to your life? OR How will you apply this to your life?

_____

_____

_____

_____

_____

They say, "when praises go up, blessings come down." Christianity is all about a blessing coming down before a praise went up.

Reflection: What does this mean to you?

_____

_____

_____

_____

_____

Application: How can you apply this to your life? OR How will you apply this to your life?

_____

_____

_____

_____

_____

Jesus is returning soon, and we must be ready. He is coming for a people who desires Him more than the garbage this world has to offer. The people of God need to look to Jesus and be sanctified from this perverse generation.

Reflection: What does this mean to you?

_____

_____

_____

_____

_____

Application: How can you apply this to your life? OR How will you apply this to your life?

_____

_____

_____

_____

_____

There are no superstars in the Kingdom of God. Look to
Jesus who is the Author and Finisher of our faith.

Reflection: What does this mean to you?

_____

_____

_____

_____

_____

Application: How can you apply this to your life? OR How will you apply
this to your life?

_____

_____

_____

_____

_____

Don't make life all about you. This is not what Jesus died for.

Reflection: What does this mean to you?

_____

_____

_____

_____

_____

_____

Application: How can you apply this to your life? OR How will you apply this to your life?

_____

_____

_____

_____

_____

_____

> Do not lose yourself trying to please them;
> lose yourself trying to please Him.

Reflection: What does this mean to you?

_____

_____

_____

_____

_____

_____

Application: How can you apply this to your life? OR How will you apply this to your life?

_____

_____

_____

_____

_____

_____

Name the sin, Jesus is greater. Name the sin, Jesus is better.

Reflection: What does this mean to you?

_____

_____

_____

_____

_____

_____

Application: How can you apply this to your life? OR How will you apply this to your life?

_____

_____

_____

_____

_____

Life without Jesus is like a body with no soul... Lifeless.

Reflection: What does this mean to you?

_____

_____

_____

_____

_____

Application: How can you apply this to your life? OR How will you apply this to your life?

_____

_____

_____

_____

_____

# Marriage

Proverbs 20:6-7
6 Many claim to have unfailing love, but a faithful person who can find?
7 The righteous lead blameless lives; blessed
are their children after them.

Marriage is an institution that has been establish by God (Gen. 2:22-24). It is a sacred covenant between a man and a woman. God instituted marriage to demonstrate the relationship Christ has for his church. It is the husband's role to lay down his life for his wife, and it is the wife's responsibility to submit to the leadership of her husband. However, we see that many marriages fail because couples are not walking in their God ordained assignment. I have been married for 9 years to my lovely wife, Pascalle. I believe the reason we are experiencing a successful marriage is because we have submitted ourselves to God's design for marriage.

Are you experiencing some ups and downs in your marriage? Do you desire a transformation in your relationship? This chapter will offer you Godly principles, of which will take your relationship to the next dimension. We are living in a time where divorce is running rampant in the world. If we are willing to fight for our marriages by getting spiritual wisdom, I believe we will encounter a revival in our relationships. Take this journey with me as we partake in Lyfe-isms for marriage.

We need to fight for our marriages because SATAN IS!

Reflection: What does this mean to you?

_____

_____

_____

_____

_____

_____

Application: How can you apply this to your life? OR How will you apply this to your life?

_____

_____

_____

_____

_____

You can only have a successful marriage when you agree to die to self.

Reflection: What does this mean to you?

_____

_____

_____

_____

_____

_____

Application: How can you apply this to your life? OR How will you apply this to your life?

_____

_____

_____

_____

_____

Build your marriage on the Word of Christ.

Reflection: What does this mean to you?

_____

_____

_____

_____

_____

_____

Application: How can you apply this to your life? OR How will you apply this to your life?

_____

_____

_____

_____

_____

Husbands, humble thyself.

Reflection: What does this mean to you?

_____

_____

_____

_____

_____

Application: How can you apply this to your life? OR How will you apply this to your life?

_____

_____

_____

_____

_____

Wives, let your words be seasoned with grace.

Reflection: What does this mean to you?

_____

_____

_____

_____

_____

_____

Application: How can you apply this to your life? OR How will you apply this to your life?

_____

_____

_____

_____

_____

_____

Your marriage ought to
exemplify the testimony of Jesus.

Reflection: What does this mean to you?

_____

_____

_____

_____

_____

_____

Application: How can you apply this to your life? OR How will you apply this to your life?

_____

_____

_____

_____

_____

_____

Saturate your home with prayer.

Reflection: What does this mean to you?

_____

_____

_____

_____

_____

_____

Application: How can you apply this to your life? OR How will you apply this to your life?

_____

_____

_____

_____

_____

Quitting should not be a consideration.

Reflection: What does this mean to you?

_____

_____

_____

_____

_____

Application: How can you apply this to your life? OR How will you apply this to your life?

_____

_____

_____

_____

_____

Compromising is for the mature.

Reflection: What does this mean to you?

_____

_____

_____

_____

_____

_____

Application: How can you apply this to your life? OR How will you apply this to your life?

_____

_____

_____

_____

_____

Love. Learn. Live. Sums it all up.

Reflection: What does this mean to you?

_____

_____

_____

_____

_____

_____

Application: How can you apply this to your life? OR How will you apply this to your life?

_____

_____

_____

_____

_____

_____

# Forgiveness

Mark 11:25 And when you stand praying, if you hold anything against anyone, forgive them, so that your Father in heaven may forgive you your sins."

The concept of forgiveness is not exclusive to the Christian community. The truth of the matter is, everyone has either extended forgiveness or received it at some point in time. Forgiveness is a big deal in the eyes of God. In order for Him to have accepted us into His family, forgiveness had to transpire. He sent His Son, Jesus Christ, to die for us. By his shed blood, He pardoned those who would trust in the finished work of Christ.

Some years ago, I started a forgiveness movement called, "The Let It Go Campaign." This movement was birthed out of my reluctance to let go of certain offenses. What I have learned throughout this movement, as I conducted conferences, was that many people shared in this struggle. When one walks in the reality that Christ forgave them, only then can they experience the freedom of forgiveness. This is more than enough reason to extend forgiveness to those around us. Let us explore this concept of letting it go and anticipate a breakthrough as we learn the implications of forgiveness.

Don't let un-forgiveness suffocate your progress. You have the power to purge it out your life. Be free in Jesus' name. There are many blessings awaiting you on the other side of forgiveness.

Reflection: What does this mean to you?

_____

_____

_____

_____

_____

Application: How can you apply this to your life? OR How will you apply this to your life?

_____

_____

_____

_____

_____

Sometimes, the most difficult person to forgive, is yourself.
Don't let your past blind you from where God has you.


Reflection: What does this mean to you?

_____

_____

_____

_____

_____

_____


Application: How can you apply this to your life? OR How will you apply
this to your life?

_____

_____

_____

_____

_____

_____

Forgiveness is the call for everyone, if you desire to be
made whole. I know they violated you and misused you,
but if you want to grow, you have to let it go.


Reflection: What does this mean to you?

_____

_____

_____

_____

_____

_____


Application: How can you apply this to your life? OR How will you apply
this to your life?

_____

_____

_____

_____

_____

_____

It's not that you can't forgive,
you just choose not to forgive.

Reflection: What does this mean to you?

_____

_____

_____

_____

_____

_____

Application: How can you apply this to your life? OR How will you apply
this to your life?

_____

_____

_____

_____

_____

When you forgive, you echo what
God has already done through Christ.

Reflection: What does this mean to you?

_____

_____

_____

_____

_____

Application: How can you apply this to your life? OR How will you apply this to your life?

_____

_____

_____

_____

_____

ABCs of Forgiveness

Admit forgiveness needs to take place.
Become an initiator of forgiveness.
Commit to loving again.


Reflection: What does this mean to you?

_____

_____

_____

_____

_____

_____


Application: How can you apply this to your life? OR How will you apply this to your life?

_____

_____

_____

_____

_____

# Intimacy
# with Christ

John 15:4

**4** Remain in me, as I also remain in you. No branch can
bear fruit by itself; it must remain in the vine. Neither
can you bear fruit unless you remain in me.

When we speak of intimacy with Christ we are referring to the solitary time spent with Him. Some people choose to wake up early in the morning and devote their waking hours in prayer and the reading of the Bible. The results of being intimate with Christ produces oneness with Him. Jesus told his disciples. "I am the vine; you are the branches. If you remain in me and I in you, you will bear much fruit; apart from me you can do nothing (John 15:5)." The key to a successful and fruitful life is when we stay connected to Christ.

In this section of Lyfe-isms, you will find inspirational principles that will encourage your consecrated walk with the Lord. I have experienced some dry spiritual seasons in my life and realized each time this occurred, I had to reevaluate how much time I was spending with Jesus. My prayer is that you will be reignited in your passion for the Lord Jesus, as you engage in a deeper level of communion with your Maker

Make your life tell His story.

Reflection: What does this mean to you?

_____

_____

_____

_____

_____

_____

Application: How can you apply this to your life? OR How will you apply this to your life?

_____

_____

_____

_____

_____

_____

Promote Jesus and
He'll promote you.

Reflection: What does this mean to you?

_____

_____

_____

_____

_____

Application: How can you apply this to your life? OR How will you apply this to your life?

_____

_____

_____

_____

_____

The more you worship Jesus,
sin becomes less desirable.

Reflection: What does this mean to you?

_____

_____

_____

_____

_____

_____

Application: How can you apply this to your life? OR How will you apply
this to your life?

_____

_____

_____

_____

_____

_____

When you walk in the fear of the Lord, you will hate
what God hates and love what God loves.


Reflection: What does this mean to you?

_____

_____

_____

_____

_____


Application: How can you apply this to your life? OR How will you apply
this to your life?

_____

_____

_____

_____

_____

Let your life be a stage where God
can perform His great works.

Reflection: What does this mean to you?

_____

_____

_____

_____

_____

_____

Application: How can you apply this to your life? OR How will you apply
this to your life?

_____

_____

_____

_____

_____

_____

The more time you spend with Jesus,
the more you resemble Him.

Reflection: What does this mean to you?

_____

_____

_____

_____

_____

Application: How can you apply this to your life? OR How will you apply this to your life?

_____

_____

_____

_____

_____

The Bible is God's holy Word to mankind. Read it and
allow it to transform your passions and desires.

Reflection: What does this mean to you?

_____

_____

_____

_____

_____

_____

Application: How can you apply this to your life? OR How will you apply
this to your life?

_____

_____

_____

_____

_____

Live with the intention to point people to
Jesus. After all, life is but a vapor.

Reflection: What does this mean to you?

_____

_____

_____

_____

_____

Application: How can you apply this to your life? OR How will you apply
this to your life?

_____

_____

_____

_____

_____

Allow Jesus to be Lord over your thoughts, speech, and
actions. We must learn to daily submit ourselves, and
the members of our bodies, to His standards.


Reflection: What does this mean to you?

_____

_____

_____

_____

_____

_____


Application: How can you apply this to your life? OR How will you apply
this to your life?

_____

_____

_____

_____

_____

_____

Can we commit to spending
more time with Jesus?

Reflection: What does this mean to you?

_____

_____

_____

_____

_____

Application: How can you apply this to your life? OR How will you apply
this to your life?

_____

_____

_____

_____

_____

Don't neglect the reading/hearing of God's Word today. It
may just keep you from living outside of your purpose.

Reflection: What does this mean to you?

_____

_____

_____

_____

_____

_____

Application: How can you apply this to your life? OR How will you apply
this to your life?

_____

_____

_____

_____

_____

_____

If you don't get in the Word,
the world will get into you.


Reflection: What does this mean to you?

_____

_____

_____

_____

_____


Application: How can you apply this to your life? OR How will you apply
this to your life?

_____

_____

_____

_____

_____

Have an encounter with Jesus today.
His presence is everything.

Reflection: What does this mean to you?

_____

_____

_____

_____

_____

_____

Application: How can you apply this to your life? OR How will you apply
this to your life?

_____

_____

_____

_____

_____

_____

I ain't tryna pleaze u, homey...
I'm just tryna please my savior only!

Reflection: What does this mean to you?

_____

_____

_____

_____

_____

Application: How can you apply this to your life? OR How will you apply this to your life?

_____

_____

_____

_____

_____

I'm learning to embrace that living in light of
the fear of God, isn't a popular stance.

Reflection: What does this mean to you?

_____

_____

_____

_____

_____

_____

Application: How can you apply this to your life? OR How will you apply
this to your life?

_____

_____

_____

_____

_____

_____

Jesus loves you passionately and He desires an
authentic relationship with you.

Reflection: What does this mean to you?

_____

_____

_____

_____

_____

Application: How can you apply this to your life? OR How will you apply
this to your life?

_____

_____

_____

_____

_____

Instead of wasting time, invest it.

Reflection: What does this mean to you?

_____

_____

_____

_____

_____

_____

Application: How can you apply this to your life? OR How will you apply this to your life?

_____

_____

_____

_____

_____

Do not love what you do,
more than you love Him.

Reflection: What does this mean to you?

_____

_____

_____

_____

_____

Application: How can you apply this to your life? OR How will you apply this to your life?

_____

_____

_____

_____

_____

The only thing that matters in
this life is the pursuit of Jesus.

Reflection: What does this mean to you?

_____

_____

_____

_____

_____

_____

Application: How can you apply this to your life? OR How will you apply
this to your life?

_____

_____

_____

_____

_____

_____

Independent living can
lead to self-destruction.


Reflection: What does this mean to you?

_____

_____

_____

_____

_____

_____


Application: How can you apply this to your life? OR How will you apply
this to your life?

_____

_____

_____

_____

_____

Worship is more than hands lifted and a song on our
lips. It is a submitted life to the lordship of Jesus.

Reflection: What does this mean to you?

_____

_____

_____

_____

_____

_____

Application: How can you apply this to your life? OR How will you apply
this to your life?

_____

_____

_____

_____

_____

Be careful to not love the song,
more than the One you are singing to.


Reflection: What does this mean to you?

_____

_____

_____

_____

_____


Application: How can you apply this to your life? OR How will you apply this to your life?

_____

_____

_____

_____

_____

Unity + Sanctity= Glory.

Reflection: What does this mean to you?

_____

_____

_____

_____

_____

_____

Application: How can you apply this to your life? OR How will you apply this to your life?

_____

_____

_____

_____

_____

_____

If we were to listen to that initial gut feeling, we
would be much further than where we are.

Reflection: What does this mean to you?

_____

_____

_____

_____

_____

Application: How can you apply this to your life? OR How will you apply
this to your life?

_____

_____

_____

_____

_____

Sin keeps you from
discovering the real you.

Reflection: What does this mean to you?

_____

_____

_____

_____

_____

_____

Application: How can you apply this to your life? OR How will you apply
this to your life?

_____

_____

_____

_____

_____

_____

The truth is, if you do not have Jesus Christ ruling
your life, you are just a dead man walking.

Reflection: What does this mean to you?

_____

_____

_____

_____

_____

_____

Application: How can you apply this to your life? OR How will you apply
this to your life?

_____

_____

_____

_____

_____

_____

Don't get it twisted,
we're all in need of a Savior.

Reflection: What does this mean to you?

_____

_____

_____

_____

_____

Application: How can you apply this to your life? OR How will you apply
this to your life?

_____

_____

_____

_____

_____

You will never know who you are,
until you know who God is.


Reflection: What does this mean to you?

_____

_____

_____

_____

_____


Application: How can you apply this to your life? OR How will you apply
this to your life?

_____

_____

_____

_____

_____

A soul is worth more than gold.

Reflection: What does this mean to you?

_____

_____

_____

_____

_____

_____

Application: How can you apply this to your life? OR How will you apply this to your life?

_____

_____

_____

_____

_____

_____

God doesn't have favorites. Why do we?

Reflection: What does this mean to you?

_____

_____

_____

_____

_____

Application: How can you apply this to your life? OR How will you apply this to your life?

_____

_____

_____

_____

_____

When you truly start walking with Jesus, many
will truly stop walking with you.

Reflection: What does this mean to you?

_____

_____

_____

_____

_____

Application: How can you apply this to your life? OR How will you apply
this to your life?

_____

_____

_____

_____

_____

Greatness is birthed out of solitary
time spent with the Father.

Reflection: What does this mean to you?

_____

_____

_____

_____

_____

Application: How can you apply this to your life? OR How will you apply
this to your life?

_____

_____

_____

_____

_____

Jesus said, "If I be lifted up, I will draw all men unto me." All we need to do is the lifting. He promised to do the drawing.

Reflection: What does this mean to you?

_____

_____

_____

_____

_____

_____

Application: How can you apply this to your life? OR How will you apply this to your life?

_____

_____

_____

_____

_____

_____

By you fulfilling your purpose, it should
encourage others to operate in theirs.


Reflection: What does this mean to you?

_____

_____

_____

_____

_____


Application: How can you apply this to your life? OR How will you apply
this to your life?

_____

_____

_____

_____

_____

When we depend on ourselves to get by,
this grieves the heart of God.

Reflection: What does this mean to you?

_____

_____

_____

_____

_____

Application: How can you apply this to your life? OR How will you apply this to your life?

_____

_____

_____

_____

_____

I refuse to live life showing people how great I am. I rather live life pointing people to the Great I Am.

Reflection: What does this mean to you?

_____
_____
_____
_____
_____
_____

Application: How can you apply this to your life? OR How will you apply this to your life?

_____
_____
_____
_____
_____

They hate you because you resemble Jesus.

Reflection: What does this mean to you?

_____

_____

_____

_____

_____

_____

Application: How can you apply this to your life? OR How will you apply this to your life?

_____

_____

_____

_____

_____

God determines whether you are
fruitful or not; not man.

Reflection: What does this mean to you?

_____

_____

_____

_____

_____

Application: How can you apply this to your life? OR How will you apply
this to your life?

_____

_____

_____

_____

_____

God never invites you to know who He is,
without letting you know, who you are.

Reflection: What does this mean to you?

_____

_____

_____

_____

_____

Application: How can you apply this to your life? OR How will you apply
this to your life?

_____

_____

_____

_____

_____

# Patience

Habakkuk 2:3 For the revelation awaits an appointed time; it speaks of the end and will not prove false. Though it linger, wait for it; it will certainly come and will not delay.

"Patience is an attribute that many fail to possess. It does not come easily. The scripture teaches that we are to consider it joy when we go through trials, because it is bringing about patience in our lives (James 1:2-3). Most of us would not have gained this virtue, had it not been for the trouble we have overcome. What I love about God, is that He doesn't give us trials and situations to break us. He uses trials to produce in us Christ-like characteristics, of which patience is one.

This portion of Lyfe-isms is power-packed with lines that will accompany you through trying seasons. Allow these words to become your "Lyfelines" as you experience the grace to continue this race.

Wait on God. He is always on time. He keeps
His promises to His beloved children.

Reflection: What does this mean to you?

_____

_____

_____

_____

_____

Application: How can you apply this to your life? OR How will you apply
this to your life?

_____

_____

_____

_____

_____

It is God's desire that we remain patient while undergoing various trails. Do not be quick to ask Him to deliver you from what you're going through. It is *all* working for your good.

Reflection: What does this mean to you?

_____

_____

_____

_____

_____

Application: How can you apply this to your life? OR How will you apply this to your life?

_____

_____

_____

_____

_____

Take notes as you experience difficulties.
There is much to learn.

Reflection: What does this mean to you?

_____

_____

_____

_____

_____

Application: How can you apply this to your life? OR How will you apply this to your life?

_____

_____

_____

_____

_____

You may not understand it all,
but God is in control.

Reflection: What does this mean to you?

_____

_____

_____

_____

_____

Application: How can you apply this to your life? OR How will you apply this to your life?

_____

_____

_____

_____

_____

# Wisdom

Proverbs 37:30 The mouths of the righteous utter
wisdom, and their tongues speak what is just.

We need knowledge to understand an idea. But without wisdom, all of your knowledge is in vain. You cannot live this life the way God intends, apart from His wisdom. The theme of Lyfe-isms is found in Proverbs 19:20, where it states, "Listen to advice and accept discipline, and at the end you will be counted among the wise." My purpose in writing Lyfe-isms is to pass down godly wisdom I have accumulated as a pastor, son, husband and father.

If I could go back in time, I would have heeded the instructions of my parents and elders. Their lessons would have kept me from unnecessary mishaps in life. I thank God that He saved my life. He not only gave me a desire for wisdom, but an aspiration to pass it down to my generation and the ones to come. You will discover in this closing chapter, random quotes which will add to your character, as it pertains to wisdom. My hope is that by reading these gems, you would not have to experience the mistakes I have made, but rather be counted among the wise.

Because it's an open door,
doesn't mean you should walk through it.

Reflection: What does this mean to you?

_____

_____

_____

_____

_____

Application: How can you apply this to your life? OR How will you apply this to your life?

_____

_____

_____

_____

_____

Broken vessels, cut people.

Reflection: What does this mean to you?

_____

_____

_____

_____

_____

_____

Application: How can you apply this to your life? OR How will you apply this to your life?

_____

_____

_____

_____

_____

Cultivate godly relationships. It will keep you
from making unfavorable decisions.

Reflection: What does this mean to you?

_____

_____

_____

_____

_____

Application: How can you apply this to your life? OR How will you apply
this to your life?

_____

_____

_____

_____

_____

Without spiritual leaders,
people revert to detrimental behavior.

Reflection: What does this mean to you?

_____

_____

_____

_____

_____

_____

Application: How can you apply this to your life? OR How will you apply this to your life?

_____

_____

_____

_____

_____

_____

True worship ought to change... you.

Reflection: What does this mean to you?

_____

_____

_____

_____

_____

_____

Application: How can you apply this to your life? OR How will you apply this to your life?

_____

_____

_____

_____

_____

_____

Do what God called you to do;
someone's life depends on it.

Reflection: What does this mean to you?

_____

_____

_____

_____

_____

_____

Application: How can you apply this to your life? OR How will you apply
this to your life?

_____

_____

_____

_____

_____

_____

You cannot manipulate pure motives.

Reflection: What does this mean to you?

_____

_____

_____

_____

_____

_____

Application: How can you apply this to your life? OR How will you apply this to your life?

_____

_____

_____

_____

_____

Usually, when your aim is to make heaven smile,
you indirectly make others frown.

Reflection: What does this mean to you?

_____

_____

_____

_____

_____

_____

Application: How can you apply this to your life? OR How will you apply
this to your life?

_____

_____

_____

_____

_____

Some people are so concerned with adorning the outward man,
while the inward man is perishing. We have it backwards.

Reflection: What does this mean to you?

_____

_____

_____

_____

_____

Application: How can you apply this to your life? OR How will you apply
this to your life?

_____

_____

_____

_____

_____

It is one thing to establish a sanctuary (Temple). But, it
is another thing to establish a people (Temple).

Reflection: What does this mean to you?

_____

_____

_____

_____

_____

_____

Application: How can you apply this to your life? OR How will you apply
this to your life?

_____

_____

_____

_____

_____

This is what the Lord calls a thing or a person that cannot produce: *a curse*. Lord, help our churches, communities, and lives to be producers and not consumers only.

Reflection: What does this mean to you?

_____

_____

_____

_____

_____

Application: How can you apply this to your life? OR How will you apply this to your life?

_____

_____

_____

_____

_____

Quick question to ponder:
Why live in darkness when the "Son" is out?

Reflection: What does this mean to you?

_____

_____

_____

_____

_____

_____

Application: How can you apply this to your life? OR How will you apply this to your life?

_____

_____

_____

_____

_____

_____

No weapon formed against a
"United People" can prosper.


Reflection: What does this mean to you?

_____

_____

_____

_____

_____

_____


Application: How can you apply this to your life? OR How will you apply this to your life?

_____

_____

_____

_____

_____

Don't look for likes,
look for God's approval.

Reflection: What does this mean to you?

_____

_____

_____

_____

_____

_____

Application: How can you apply this to your life? OR How will you apply
this to your life?

_____

_____

_____

_____

_____

# Honor

Romans 12:10 Love one another with brotherly affection. Outdo one another in showing honor.

Honor is a trait that we all must possess. We live in a time when dishonor is running rampant. In order to cultivate any lasting and fulfilled relationship we must embrace the honor principle. The scripture speaks a great deal on the topic of honor. If is close to the heart of God, then it ought to be close to ours as well.

In this chapter, you will encounter several quotes on the topic of honor. My hope is that it encourages you and compels you to live an honorable life. May these quotes come alive to you, and grant you revelation from above.

Honor must be seen, not heard.

Reflection: What does this mean to you?

_____

_____

_____

_____

_____

Application: How can you apply this to your life? OR How will you apply this to your life?

_____

_____

_____

_____

_____

Use your words to edify, not to destroy.

Reflection: What does this mean to you?

_____

_____

_____

_____

_____

_____

Application: How can you apply this to your life? OR How will you apply this to your life?

_____

_____

_____

_____

_____

When you honor God, He honors you.

Reflection: What does this mean to you?

_____

_____

_____

_____

_____

Application: How can you apply this to your life? OR How will you apply this to your life?

_____

_____

_____

_____

_____

Don't treat the uncommon thing as common.

Reflection: What does this mean to you?

_____

_____

_____

_____

_____

_____

Application: How can you apply this to your life? OR How will you apply this to your life?

_____

_____

_____

_____

_____

_____

Allow God to sanctify your convictions.

Reflection: What does this mean to you?

_____

_____

_____

_____

_____

Application: How can you apply this to your life? OR How will you apply this to your life?

_____

_____

_____

_____

_____

Honor unlocks blessings and breakthrough.

Reflection: What does this mean to you?

_____

_____

_____

_____

_____

_____

Application: How can you apply this to your life? OR How will you apply this to your life?

_____

_____

_____

_____

_____

When you choose Honor,
you choose to be rewarded.

Reflection: What does this mean to you?

_____

_____

_____

_____

_____

_____

Application: How can you apply this to your life? OR How will you apply this to your life?

_____

_____

_____

_____

_____

When you are tested,
what you honor will be evident.


Reflection: What does this mean to you?

_____

_____

_____

_____

_____

_____


Application: How can you apply this to your life? OR How will you apply this to your life?

_____

_____

_____

_____

_____

Honor should be the first response,
not an alternative reaction.


Reflection: What does this mean to you?

_____

_____

_____

_____

_____


Application: How can you apply this to your life? OR How will you apply this to your life?

_____

_____

_____

_____

_____

Familiarity is your worst enemy.

Reflection: What does this mean to you?

_____

_____

_____

_____

_____

Application: How can you apply this to your life? OR How will you apply this to your life?

_____

_____

_____

_____

_____

Honoring comes by revelation,
not information.


Reflection: What does this mean to you?

_____

_____

_____

_____

_____

_____


Application: How can you apply this to your life? OR How will you apply
this to your life?

_____

_____

_____

_____

_____

When you fail to honor,
you miss an opportunity to grow.

Reflection: What does this mean to you?

_____

_____

_____

_____

_____

Application: How can you apply this to your life? OR How will you apply
this to your life?

_____

_____

_____

_____

_____

Be careful who you partner with.

Reflection: What does this mean to you?

_____

_____

_____

_____

_____

_____

Application: How can you apply this to your life? OR How will you apply this to your life?

_____

_____

_____

_____

_____

To Honor Man is to Honor God.

Reflection: What does this mean to you?

_____

_____

_____

_____

_____

_____

Application: How can you apply this to your life? OR How will you apply this to your life?

_____

_____

_____

_____

_____

In the same way, honor has a reward system,
dishonor has a reward system.


Reflection: What does this mean to you?

_____

_____

_____

_____

_____

_____


Application: How can you apply this to your life? OR How will you apply this to your life?

_____

_____

_____

_____

_____

When you don't know the
value of something, you will dishonor it.

Reflection: What does this mean to you?

_____

_____

_____

_____

_____

_____

Application: How can you apply this to your life? OR How will you apply
this to your life?

_____

_____

_____

_____

_____

_____

Dishonor short-circuit blessings
and the flow of God over you.


Reflection: What does this mean to you?

_____

_____

_____

_____

_____


Application: How can you apply this to your life? OR How will you apply this to your life?

_____

_____

_____

_____

_____

Your heart for God should
lead to honoring down.

Reflection: What does this mean to you?

_____

_____

_____

_____

_____

Application: How can you apply this to your life? OR How will you apply this to your life?

_____

_____

_____

_____

_____

When you underestimate someone,
you miss an opportunity to honor them.


Reflection: What does this mean to you?

_____

_____

_____

_____

_____

_____


Application: How can you apply this to your life? OR How will you apply this to your life?

_____

_____

_____

_____

_____

_____

Honoring down is a picture of
what Christ has done for us.

Reflection: What does this mean to you?

_____

_____

_____

_____

_____

_____

Application: How can you apply this to your life? OR How will you apply
this to your life?

_____

_____

_____

_____

_____

Don't ever be so high that you
forget to consider down.


Reflection: What does this mean to you?

_____

_____

_____

_____

_____

_____


Application: How can you apply this to your life? OR How will you apply
this to your life?

_____

_____

_____

_____

_____

Love the person, not just the gift.

Reflection: What does this mean to you?

_____

_____

_____

_____

_____

_____

Application: How can you apply this to your life? OR How will you apply this to your life?

_____

_____

_____

_____

_____

Give according to how you want to receive.

Reflection: What does this mean to you?

_____

_____

_____

_____

_____

_____

Application: How can you apply this to your life? OR How will you apply this to your life?

_____

_____

_____

_____

_____

Protect yourself from ungodly alliances.

Reflection: What does this mean to you?

_____

_____

_____

_____

_____

Application: How can you apply this to your life? OR How will you apply this to your life?

_____

_____

_____

_____

_____

The best way to evict dishonor is
by showing acts of kindness.


Reflection: What does this mean to you?

_____

_____

_____

_____

_____

_____


Application: How can you apply this to your life? OR How will you apply
this to your life?

_____

_____

_____

_____

_____

Honor your elders,
because they see what you don't.

Reflection: What does this mean to you?

_____

_____

_____

_____

_____

Application: How can you apply this to your life? OR How will you apply this to your life?

_____

_____

_____

_____

_____

Speak truth. Stay humble.
Honor Always.

Reflection: What does this mean to you?

_____

_____

_____

_____

_____

_____

Application: How can you apply this to your life? OR How will you apply this to your life?

_____

_____

_____

_____

_____

If they don't honor you,
change environments.

Reflection: What does this mean to you?

_____

_____

_____

_____

_____

_____

Application: How can you apply this to your life? OR How will you apply
this to your life?

_____

_____

_____

_____

_____

_____

Pride precedes dishonor.

Reflection: What does this mean to you?

_____

_____

_____

_____

_____

Application: How can you apply this to your life? OR How will you apply
this to your life?

_____

_____

_____

_____

_____

Honor your convictions.

Reflection: What does this mean to you?

_____

_____

_____

_____

_____

_____

Application: How can you apply this to your life? OR How will you apply this to your life?

_____

_____

_____

_____

_____

# Sacred Conviction

Ephesians 5:15
So be careful how you live. Don't live like fools, but like those who are wise.

C onviction is defined as such, a firmly held belief or opinion. In our walk with Christ, we must embrace certain convictions that would set us apart. Without sacred convictions, we will liken to a ship without a sail. If we don't set boundaries around our lives we will drift and ultimately wither away. In this chapter, you will encounter some convictions that, if embraced and understood properly, will add much value to your walk with God. Be inspired and empowered as you walk out your personal convictions.

Your motives hold more
weight than your actions.

Reflection: What does this mean to you?

_____

_____

_____

_____

_____

Application: How can you apply this to your life? OR How will you apply
this to your life?

_____

_____

_____

_____

_____

Idols can block you from
experiencing the presence of God.

Reflection: What does this mean to you?

_____

_____

_____

_____

_____

_____

Application: How can you apply this to your life? OR How will you apply
this to your life?

_____

_____

_____

_____

_____

_____

Humility keeps you close
to the heart of God.


Reflection: What does this mean to you?

_____

_____

_____

_____

_____


Application: How can you apply this to your life? OR How will you apply this to your life?

_____

_____

_____

_____

_____

Idols can block you from
experiencing the presence of God.

Reflection: What does this mean to you?

_____

_____

_____

_____

_____

_____

Application: How can you apply this to your life? OR How will you apply
this to your life?

_____

_____

_____

_____

_____

Your character will open doors for you.


Reflection: What does this mean to you?

_____

_____

_____

_____

_____

_____


Application: How can you apply this to your life? OR How will you apply this to your life?

_____

_____

_____

_____

_____

Contentment is the key that
unlocks peace in your life.

Reflection: What does this mean to you?

_____

_____

_____

_____

_____

Application: How can you apply this to your life? OR How will you apply
this to your life?

_____

_____

_____

_____

_____

God's will must trump the will of man.

Reflection: What does this mean to you?

_____

_____

_____

_____

_____

Application: How can you apply this to your life? OR How will you apply this to your life?

_____

_____

_____

_____

_____

The more you grow,
the more you ought to remain low.


Reflection: What does this mean to you?

_____

_____

_____

_____

_____


Application: How can you apply this to your life? OR How will you apply
this to your life?

_____

_____

_____

_____

_____

Educate yourself, empower your family,
and engage your community.


Reflection: What does this mean to you?

_____

_____

_____

_____

_____

_____


Application: How can you apply this to your life? OR How will you apply this to your life?

_____

_____

_____

_____

_____

_____

When you sanctify your thoughts,
you sanctify your decisions.

Reflection: What does this mean to you?

_____

_____

_____

_____

_____

Application: How can you apply this to your life? OR How will you apply this to your life?

_____

_____

_____

_____

_____

Your life should be marked by serving others.


Reflection: What does this mean to you?

_____

_____

_____

_____

_____

_____


Application: How can you apply this to your life? OR How will you apply this to your life?

_____

_____

_____

_____

_____

_____

Pray daily, listen carefully,
and move cautiously.

Reflection: What does this mean to you?

_____

_____

_____

_____

_____

Application: How can you apply this to your life? OR How will you apply this to your life?

_____

_____

_____

_____

_____

Social media can be
kryptonite if you allow it.


Reflection: What does this mean to you?

_____

_____

_____

_____

_____


Application: How can you apply this to your life? OR How will you apply
this to your life?

_____

_____

_____

_____

_____

Don't do it for the applause,
do it for the cause.

Reflection: What does this mean to you?

_____

_____

_____

_____

_____

_____

Application: How can you apply this to your life? OR How will you apply
this to your life?

_____

_____

_____

_____

_____

_____

Don't let what they said to keep you
from living up to what He said.

Reflection: What does this mean to you?

_____

_____

_____

_____

_____

_____

Application: How can you apply this to your life? OR How will you apply this to your life?

_____

_____

_____

_____

_____

Don't let reading the
Bible become a rare art.

Reflection: What does this mean to you?

_____

_____

_____

_____

_____

_____

Application: How can you apply this to your life? OR How will you apply
this to your life?

_____

_____

_____

_____

_____

_____

If you see it, address it.

Reflection: What does this mean to you?

_____

_____

_____

_____

_____

_____

Application: How can you apply this to your life? OR How will you apply this to your life?

_____

_____

_____

_____

_____

_____

Never leave someone's presence
without sowing a seed.

Reflection: What does this mean to you?

_____

_____

_____

_____

_____

Application: How can you apply this to your life? OR How will you apply
this to your life?

_____

_____

_____

_____

_____

Before you say it,
make sure you can back it up.

Reflection: What does this mean to you?

_____

_____

_____

_____

_____

Application: How can you apply this to your life? OR How will you apply
this to your life?

_____

_____

_____

_____

_____

Idleness hinders productivity.

Reflection: What does this mean to you?

_____

_____

_____

_____

_____

_____

Application: How can you apply this to your life? OR How will you apply this to your life?

_____

_____

_____

_____

_____

Allow God to define you,
not your present circumstance.

Reflection: What does this mean to you?

_____

_____

_____

_____

_____

Application: How can you apply this to your life? OR How will you apply
this to your life?

_____

_____

_____

_____

_____

Think before forming alliances.

Reflection: What does this mean to you?

_____

_____

_____

_____

_____

_____

Application: How can you apply this to your life? OR How will you apply this to your life?

_____

_____

_____

_____

_____

Be still until God reveals His will.


Reflection: What does this mean to you?

_____

_____

_____

_____

_____


Application: How can you apply this to your life? OR How will you apply this to your life?

_____

_____

_____

_____

_____

The smaller your circle,
the lesser the anxiety.

Reflection: What does this mean to you?

_____

_____

_____

_____

_____

_____

Application: How can you apply this to your life? OR How will you apply this to your life?

_____

_____

_____

_____

_____

Don't give your emotional
stability to anyone.


Reflection: What does this mean to you?

_____

_____

_____

_____

_____

_____


Application: How can you apply this to your life? OR How will you apply this to your life?

_____

_____

_____

_____

_____

Time always reveals true motives.

Reflection: What does this mean to you?

_____

_____

_____

_____

_____

_____

Application: How can you apply this to your life? OR How will you apply this to your life?

_____

_____

_____

_____

_____

_____

Don't take on a load that
wasn't meant for you.

Reflection: What does this mean to you?

_____

_____

_____

_____

_____

Application: How can you apply this to your life? OR How will you apply this to your life?

_____

_____

_____

_____

_____

Spirituality is Practicality.


Reflection: What does this mean to you?

_____

_____

_____

_____

_____

_____


Application: How can you apply this to your life? OR How will you apply this to your life?

_____

_____

_____

_____

_____

_____

Steward your ideas well.

Reflection: What does this mean to you?

_____

_____

_____

_____

_____

Application: How can you apply this to your life? OR How will you apply this to your life?

_____

_____

_____

_____

_____

Speak the truth even if it's uncomfortable.

Reflection: What does this mean to you?

_____

_____

_____

_____

_____

_____

Application: How can you apply this to your life? OR How will you apply this to your life?

_____

_____

_____

_____

_____

Don't allow what is happening
around you to consume you.

Reflection: What does this mean to you?

_____

_____

_____

_____

_____

_____

Application: How can you apply this to your life? OR How will you apply
this to your life?

_____

_____

_____

_____

_____

If you want God to do a new thing,
you must let go of the old thing.

Reflection: What does this mean to you?

_____

_____

_____

_____

_____

Application: How can you apply this to your life? OR How will you apply this to your life?

_____

_____

_____

_____

_____

www.ingramcontent.com/pod-product-compliance
Lightning Source LLC
Chambersburg PA
CBHW021625120626
46545CB00002B/394